HOW TO RIDE A UNICYCLE

Jack Wiley

ISBN-13: 978-1508554219
ISBN-10: 1508554218

CONTENTS

INTRODUCTION

It is sometimes said that "anyone can ride a unicycle," but in actual fact it takes a very special person. Both a desire to learn and a certain fitness level are essential. A unicycle is also required.

It is an established fact, however, that many people possess these qualifications. Conservative estimates are that at least 100,000 people have learned to ride a unicycle!

Once confined mainly to professional performers, unicycling is now a rapidly growing recreational activity and competitive sport. The Unicycle Society of America has held a National Unicycle Meet annually since 1973; and the International Unicycling Federation now sponsors world championships with participants from a number of countries.

Quality manufactured unicycles are now readily available in a price range from about $75 to $180. Many people want to learn to ride a unicycle, but do not know how to go about it.

I have seen many methods used for learning to ride unicycles. While most result in learning to ride, some work much better than others. Many people have learned to ride by trial and error, without any instruction. This method (or lack of method) often works, but it has a number of drawbacks, especially that it often isn't the safest way to learn, it can lead to bad riding habits that can be difficult to correct later, it can be damaging to unicycles, and it can take an unnecessarily long time.

The step-by-step method detailed in this book has proven to be efficient and result in good riding techniques.

This book is intended as a complete guide for the novice who wants to learn to ride a standard unicycle and then perform basic skills such as mounting, turning, and riding with a partner; and for those who want to teach others to ride and perform basic skills.

Chapter 1

BASIC PRINCIPLES

Over the years a variety of types, sizes, and designs of one-wheel cycles have been built and ridden. The most common and popular design (and the one of concern in this book) is the basic standard unicycle (Figure 1-1).

For our purposes here, a "unicycle" is defined as a one-wheel cycle that has the rider above the wheel. This makes balance difficult and challenging because most of the rider's weight is above the center of the wheel. Another type of one-wheel cycle has the rider inside the wheel and is often called a "monocycle" (Figure 1-2).

This book is devoted entirely to the basic standard unicycle, which is generally considered to be the best type for learning basic riding. It is also the most popular unicycle for artistic riding at all levels of skill.

However, there are many other variations of the standard unicycle, such as those shown along with a basic saddle model in Figure 1-3, and giraffe unicycles, such as the basic model shown in Figure 1-4, that you may want to try after you have learned to ride a basic standard unicycle.

Figure 1-2. A monocycle has the rider inside the wheel.

Figure 1-1. A basic standard unicycle.

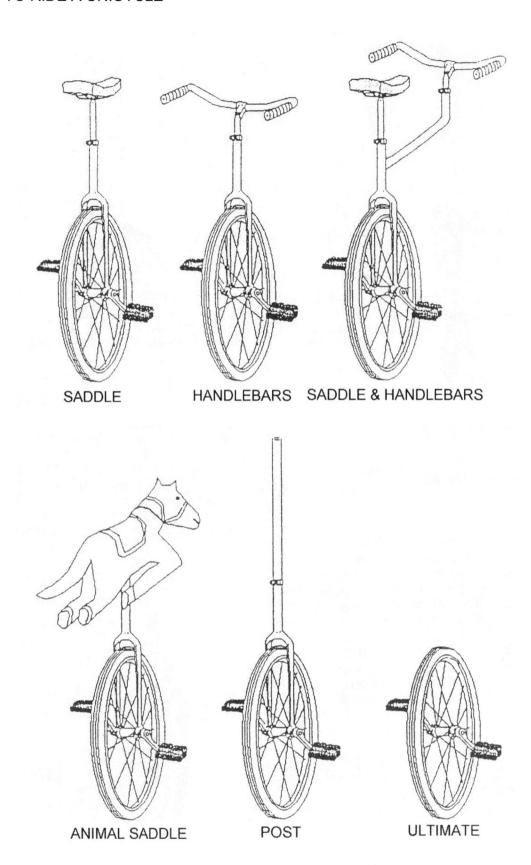

Figure 1-3. Variations of the standard unicycle.

Figure 1-4. Giraffe unicycle.

Figure 1-5. The center of gravity is above the center of the wheel.

BASIC STANDARD UNICYCLE

A basic standard unicycle has an axle that is fixed to the hub with the crank arms in turn fixed to the axle. The axle turns in bearings that are mounted on the ends of the fork prongs. A saddle is mounted on the stem end of the fork. A unicycle of this design with a 16-inch wheel is considered standard for a small child and with 20-inch and 24-inch wheels for larger riders, including adults (selection of a unicycle for learning to ride is covered in the next chapter).

MECHANICS OF UNICYCLING

Before attempting to learn to ride a unicycle, it is helpful to first understand the mechanics that make it possible to keep balance over one wheel. The basic standard unicycle, as detailed above, is not freewheeling. Since the axle and crank arms are fixed to the hub,

the turning of the wheel is controlled directly by the pedal action.

When mounted on the unicycle, most of the rider's weight and the weight of the unicycle (and the point where most of this weight is concentrated, called the "center of gravity") are above the center of the wheel or axle (Figure 1-5). When mounted on the unicycle, the area of the tire that is in contact with the ground (called the "base of support") usually isn't large enough or flat enough for the rider to maintain stationary balance, at least not easily.

How then is it possible to ride a unicycle? To answer this question, we will first consider what is required to remain in balance on a unicycle. To maintain stationary balance without the wheel turning, the center of gravity must be directly above and within the area where the tire contacts the ground. This, of course, is a difficult balance to maintain.

Unicycle riding usually involves maintaining balance while in motion. Forward and backward balance is maintained by a series of corrections. If the rider starts from a momentary stationary balance and begins to fall forward, pedaling forward forcefully enough will then cause the wheel to move forward

Figure 1-6. When balance is lost forward, correction is made by pedaling forward or increasing the speed of pedaling if already pedaling forward.

Figure 1-7. When balance is lost backward from stationary position, correction is made by pedaling backwards. When balance is lost backward while riding forward, correction is made by slowing down or reversing the pedaling.

more rapidly than the unicycle and rider are falling forward. This will restore balance (Figure 1-6).

If the rider starts from a momentary stationary balance and begins to fall backwards, pedaling backwards forcefully enough will cause the wheel to move backwards more rapidly than the unicycle and rider are falling backwards and restore balance (Figure 1-7).

When riding forward on the unicycle, forward and backward balance can usually be maintained without actually pedaling backwards by maintaining a slight forward lean and speeding up the pedal action if balance is too far forward and slowing or stopping the pedal actions if balance is too far backward.

There are times, however, when balance will be lost so far backwards that only a backward pedaling action can bring the rider forward over the balance point again. This is why both forward and backward pedaling actions should be practiced right from the start, as detailed in Chapter 3.

There are many other mechanics to unicycling, but this is all you really need to know to learn basic riding. Start practicing in

your mind. Imagine that you are on the unicycle pedaling forward and you start to lose your balance forward. The first tendency might be to bend forward and reach for the ground, but this would only serve to make you fall faster. What you should do is maintain good riding posture and pedal faster to bring the unicycle wheel up under you (see Figure 1-6).

Also imagine that you are riding forward and you start to lose your balance backwards. Again the natural response might be to bend forward at the waist and reach forward for the ground, but this won't restore your balance. What you need to do is maintain good riding posture and slow the pedaling action so that the wheel slows down, but you keep going at the same speed as previously, which serves to bring you forward in relation to the unicycle wheel (see Figure 1 7).

At this point you may be wondering why balance isn't maintained by arm and upper body movements. Actually, it can be, at least to a certain extent. However, this is minor compared to the power available to restore balance by pedal action. Besides, it is extremely difficult to make the correct arm and/or upper body movements, and random and uncontrolled movements generally do more harm than good.

It generally works best to use good riding posture without any upper body actions (see Figure 1-5). Good riding posture means that you have what would be considered good standing posture. You essentially become an extension of the unicycle, and the basic idea is to maintain this posture while you learn basic forward riding.

Another way to think about unicycling is to consider the rider and unicycle as being a pole, which you are trying to balance in the palm of your hand (Figure 1-8). If the pole starts to fall in one direction, you move your hand in the same direction to restore balance. The same principle applies to unicycling. If balance is lost in one direction, it can be restored by pedaling the wheel in that direction.

I now believe that unicyclists also have another method for maintaining forward and backward balance. Since the crank arms are anchored to the wheel, the rider has one foot forward and the other foot rearward when the cranks are in a horizontal position. This allows shifting the rider's body and the unicycle frame and saddle forward or backwards in relation to the center of the wheel. This can be done within certain limits regardless of whether the unicycle wheel is stationary or turning. This seems to make unicycling much easier than if only speeding up or slowing down or stopping or reversing the wheel were possible.

To this point, only forward and backward balance has been considered. This is what you should concentrate on when you are first learning. However, when you lose balance to the side, it can be restored similarly by turning slightly in the direction balance is being lost and then pedaling the wheel in that direction to restore balance. By the time you have learned forward and backward balance, you will probably find that you have also learned the basic technique for maintaining side-to-side balance.

The pedaling action itself tends to cause the unicycle to wobble from side to side. Experienced riders, however, keep this action to a minimum. Riding without wobbling is one of the first things you should practice after you can do basic riding.

Turning can be accomplished by leaning in the direction you wish to turn or by twisting the arms and upper body in one direction rapidly, which causes the unicycle wheel to twist in the opposite direction. Most beginners find that once they can do solo riding forward, they can already make turns.

When first attempting to learn to ride a unicycle, I have found that it works best if the rider concentrates on learning the forward and backward balance. Once forward and backward balance has been mastered, most riders already know how to maintain side-to-side balance and make turns.

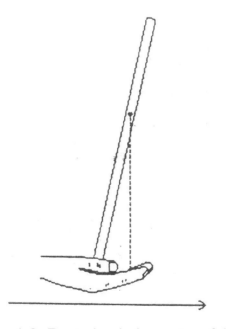

Figure 1-8. Restoring balance to a falling pole by moving your hand under it.

HOW LONG WILL IT TAKE TO LEARN TO RIDE?

This, of course, depends on many things. It depends, for example, on the physical, mental, and emotional characteristics of the person attempting to learn. It depends also on the method used for learning.

Using the step-by-step method detailed in Chapter 3, a few people have learned to ride a unicycle to the point where they could solo with reasonable control in an hour or less. However, this is the exception and not the rule. A week or more of practicing several hours a day is more typical. Some people have taken a month or even more. Certainly there are people who could never learn to ride a unicycle. But it has been my experience that nearly everyone in reasonable physical shape (and some who aren't) who has a strong desire to learn and who sticks with it can learn.

I know of one school that had riding a unicycle as a requirement for passing physical education. Every student (fourth to eighth grades, both boys and girls) learned to ride. The time that it took them to learn, however, varied widely. Some took to it quickly, others took a long time. But every student there did learn.

As a general rule, young people seem to learn most readily, but even at relatively old ages it isn't impossible.

Most people want to learn as fast as possible, but it's also important to consider safety and the development of good riding techniques. This will save time in the long run.

The length and frequency of practice sessions are important considerations. I have found that most people tend to learn faster with three or more short practice sessions a week rather than, say, one long practice session once a week. Three to five one-hour practice sessions a week seems to work well for most beginners.

Chapter 2

UNICYCLES

The most important piece of equipment that you will need is a unicycle. The type of unicycle that you need is the basic standard, as detailed in Chapter 1. Manufactured versions of these unicycles are now readily available.

MANUFACTURED UNICYCLES

A number of companies (both domestic and foreign) are presently manufacturing basic standard unicycles. It is extremely important to select what is often called a "professional model" (Figure 2-1). These are built in a manner similar to quality bicycles. They feature sturdy bearings mounted securely to the unicycle frame, an axle fixed to the hub, crank arms securely attached to the axle and an inflated tire with a tube.

Also manufactured are unicycles that are constructed along the lines of tricycles or that have some combination of both tricycle and bicycles design and construction. My experience has been that these unicycles are a waste of money. While they may hold up for a time with small children, their lack of precision makes them difficult to ride. For adults, they are not only difficult to ride, but also of inadequate strength. These unicycles generally have a much lower price tag than do "professional models," but they are generally poor economy. These unicycles will not be treated further in this book. My advice is that if you want to take up unicycling, get a "professional model" unicycle.

Recommended unicycles that are presently being manufactured include Torker, Sem-cycle, Kris Holm, Nimbus, Avenir, and Aosom. These and other suitable "professional model" unicycles are available from some bicycle shops. These unicycles presently range in price from about $75 to $180. A variety of unicycles are available from Amazon.com and other online stores.

Figure 2-1. A "professional model" basic standard unicycle.

When selecting a unicycle, you will have a choice of three basic wheel sizes: 16-inch, 20-inch, and 24-inch. I recommend the 20-inch wheel for all beginners except those too small to comfortably reach the pedals with this size, in which case I recommend the smaller 16-inch wheel.

Another important consideration is that the saddle height be adjustable for the particular rider (see next chapter). All of the manufactured unicycles mentioned above allow adjusting the saddle height, but within a limited range. You will want to make certain that the saddle can be adjusted low enough or high enough for you. In some cases, a longer seat post can be used for riders too tall for the standard length.

All of the unicycles mentioned above have curved unicycle-type saddles. A few models have metal or plastic saddle protectors, which help protect the unicycle if it is dropped.

In some cases the unicycle can be purchased fully assembled. In other cases it will be only partially assembled, such as shown in Figure 2-2. Assembly instructions are usually included.

CARE AND MAINTENANCE

With reasonable care, most well-constructed unicycles will give long service with a minimum of maintenance. Especially important is to avoid dropping the unicycle. Catching the unicycle as you dismount is one of the first skills that should be mastered when learning to ride a unicycle (see next chapter).

Unicycles should be stored inside out of extreme weather conditions to prevent rusting and other deterioration.

Unicycles usually have sealed bearings, with no additional lubrication being required.

The unicycle should be kept clean and dry. Use a cloth to wipe off dirt and moisture. Wax should be applied to painted and chrome-plated surfaces at regular intervals.

Keep all bolts properly tightened. From time to time it may be necessary to align the wheel and adjust the spokes. You can have this work done at a bicycle shop if you do not know how to do it yourself.

The tire should be kept properly inflated. Tire life can be prolonged by rotating the tire position on the rim from time to time so that twisting and turning when using the unicycle will be done on different areas of the tire.

Figure 2-2. Components of unicycle as received in shipping carton.

CLOTHING AND PROTECTIVE EQUIPMENT

Comfortable play and recreational clothing is ideal for unicycling. Shoes with heels should be worn. Athletic shoes with short heels are ideal. Do not ride barefooted.

Some riders have the problem of hitting their ankles on the crank arms when riding. One solution is to turn the ankles slightly outward. Protective rubber pads can also be used inside socks. For some riders, banging the ankles will not be a problem, in which case the protectors will not be needed.

Other protective equipment, such as knee pads, elbow pads, thick leather gloves, and helmets, can also be used.

Chapter 3

LEARNING TO RIDE

This chapter details a proven step-by-step method for learning to ride a unicycle.

ADJUSTING THE UNICYCLE

For most people, I have found that a standard unicycle with a 20-inch wheel works best. The unicycle should be of the "professional" type (see Chapter 2). Small children sometimes learn best with a unicycle with a 16-inch wheel. Most teenagers and adults can also learn on a unicycle with a 24-inch wheel, but this can make learning a little more difficult.

Before actually starting, it's important to have the unicycle properly adjusted. The saddle height is correct when, mounted on the unicycle, your leg is almost extended to reach the pedal in the down position (lowest point in relation to the ground). This should be possible, however, without having to lean the body to that side in order to keep the ball of the foot flat on the pedal. The adjustment on most unicycles is made by loosening the saddle-post clamp, sliding the post up or down in the fork stem until the saddle is the desired height, and then retightening the clamp. On some unicycles, such as the Schwinn, the saddle-adjustment bolt passes through the unicycle frame and the saddle post. To adjust to a new height, remove the bolt and move the saddle post up or down in the frame to desired height. Then insert securing bolt. It may be necessary to shift the post slightly to allow the bolt to pass through one of the adjustment holes.

Most manufactured unicycles now come with special unicycle saddles. Some of these saddles are shaped the same on both ends, making the front or back arbitrary. .

In this case, ride the unicycle with the right pedal (this is usually marked with an "R" stamped on the end of the pedal shaft) on your right side when you are facing forward. This will prevent the pedals from coming loose when riding forward. For proper riding, the end of the saddle that is used as the front should be angled slightly upward. If the unicycle saddle is shaped with a front and a back, it should be angled slightly upward toward the front for easiest riding. Some manufactured unicycle saddles allow for adjustment of the angle, others don't. Fortunately, the ones that don't are usually already mounted at the correct angles. If the saddle is not angled upward toward the front, it will tend to slip out from under the rider and steering and control will be difficult. The amount of upward angle is a matter of personal preference, but many riders find that having the front of the saddle from one to about three inches higher than the back to be about right.

To adjust the saddle angle on most unicycle saddles that allow this, loosen the clamp, tilt the saddle to the desired angle, and then retighten the clamp.

Some beginners start with a slightly under-inflated tire, which helps prevent twisting about a vertical axis. After getting the "feel" of the unicycle, the tire should be inflated to the correct pressure.

TRAINING AIDS

I have seen many different training aids used, including training poles, a ring that slides along an overhead cable, and spotting belts. I have tried these and other similar devices in my own teaching, but have concluded that they usually retard rather than aid learning at the beginning level, although they may be useful for learning more advanced skills.

There are some learning aids that I have found to be helpful, however. First, you will need a 4 x 4 inch block of wood a couple of feet long to use as a stop-block or a curb from about four to six inches high located adjacent to a suitable riding surface that will serve the same purpose. Second, you will need two partners to assist you in learning. It is not necessary that they know how to ride unicycles.

A PLACE TO LEARN

Learn on a hard smooth surface, such as asphalt, concrete, or a wooden floor. You will need a large open space. In most cases, except perhaps in a recreation room, it's best not to try to learn to ride a unicycle inside a house, at least not if the floor, furniture, and knickknacks are valued.

After learning to ride, it will no longer be necessary to be this selective as to where the unicycle is ridden. Experienced riders, for example, can ride on grass, but this is extremely difficult for a beginner and generally only serves to make learning more difficult.

Learn on a level or slightly downhill surface, but avoid an uphill grade. Again, an experienced rider can unicycle on varied terrain, but it is best to be selective for learning.

SAFETY AND PROTECTION OF UNICYCLE

In order to make learning to ride a unicycle a safe and enjoyable experience, it should be done one step at a time. Master each step before going on to the next one. It is ex-

tremely important to learn the correct techniques right from the start, including dismounting. Remember, dismounting is not falling. It's a controlled method for getting off a unicycle.

Learn to ride in an area that is free of automobile traffic and other hazards. The beginner needs to be able to concentrate fully on learning to ride the unicycle, without distractions or safety hazards to worry about.

Don't forget about the "safety" of the unicycle. Try not to drop it, as this can damage and even ruin it. Learn the correct techniques for catching the unicycle by the saddle when dismounting, as detailed below in this chapter, right from the start.

BASIC RIDING

While there are all degrees of being able to ride a unicycle, and it's possible to continue to learn new skills and techniques throughout a lifetime, we often say that a person knows how to ride a unicycle when he or she can ride solo with some degree of control.

In order to ride, a person must first mount the unicycle. The most important riding skill to master is the forward and backward balance. Once this is learned, side-to-side balance and making turns is usually fairly easy. Unicycling is possible basically because the rider has control of the wheel and thus the relationship between the wheel and unicycle frame. When the wheel gets behind the rider, the pedal action is increased so that the wheel catches up and is moved back under the rider. In turn, if the wheel gets ahead of the unicycle frame, the rider slows the pedal action so that the unicycle frame and rider catch up. Smooth forward riding is done by being slightly off balance forward and pedaling forward so that the wheel moves along at the same speed as the unicycle saddle.

One method of riding is to always be in either exact balance or off balance forward, but never off balance backwards. However, this method limits the rider to forward riding and stopping and does not allow regaining balance if balance is lost backwards or permit riding backwards.

In order to overcome these limitations, the rider needs not only to be able to pedal forward at varying speeds and to stop the pedal action, but also to be able to reverse the pedal direction and be able to pedal backwards at varying speeds. These actions greatly increase the control that the rider has in moving the unicycle wheel, and for advanced riding they are essential. It has been my experience that these techniques are best learned right from the start, before developing a forward-only-pedaling habit has been established.

In the above discussion, I have considered the unicycle frame and the rider to be a unit, but this is only true if the rider maintains good posture, with the body upright and the head and shoulders in line with the unicycle frame (Figure 3-1). Balance is usually best controlled by pedal action rather than movement of the upper body or arms. This means that the rider is a fixed extension of the unicycle frame. This is the old principle of being easier to balance a broom-stick than a flexible hose on your hand.

Learning with Two Helpers

To get started, you will need two assistants, a block of wood or curb for use as a stop-block, and a suitable riding surface. Place the unicycle wheel against the stop-block or curb (Figure 3-2). Stand behind the unicycle on the curb or behind the block of wood and tilt the unicycle back toward you. Have one pedal back toward you so that placing weight on it will force the wheel against the curb or block. With the helpers at your sides, straddle over the unicycle saddle. Hold hands with the helpers and mount the unicycle by placing foot on the pedal that is back toward you. This will be the right foot if the pedal that is back is on the right side and the left foot if the back pedal is on the left side. One position or the other will probably feel most natural, and you can deliberately place the pedals in position for this.

Step the other foot from the ground to the free pedal and allow the saddle (with your weight on it) to come up to a position over the wheel. Keep most of your weight on the pedal that is toward the curb or block to prevent the wheel from rolling forward out from under you.

Figure 3-1. Good riding posture with the body upright and the head and shoulders in line with the unicycle frame.

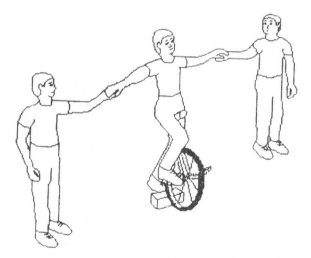

Figure 3-2. Positions for mounting unicycle with stop-block or curb and two helpers.

18

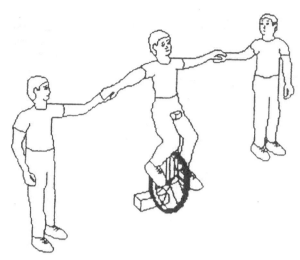

Figure 3-3. Rider mounted on unicycle with helpers standing directly to sides.

When mounted on the unicycle (Figure 3-3), have the helpers stand directly to your sides. The helpers should support you with their palms upward and they should hold your hands out so that your arms are extended to your sides. The helpers should provide side-to-side support and keep you from twisting and turning. This will allow you to concentrate on learning the forward and back-ward balance, which is the key to learning to ride a unicycle.

Begin by leaning the saddle slightly forward and making a half-pedal revolution forward (Figure 3-4). Strive to keep the saddle moving forward at the same rate as the wheel. A common mistake is to let the saddle lag behind. Take only a half pedal revolution until the crank arms are in the next horizontal position. Freeze the pedals in this position and stand up on the pedals with legs locked straight and unicycle saddle squeezed between your legs. This will make it easier for the partners to help you regain balance. The helpers should remain directly to your sides as you move along so that they can keep you from twisting and falling to the side.

After the first half-pedal revolution, regain balance and then make a second half-pedal revolution. Freeze with the pedals in the horizontal position, standing up on the pedals with the legs locked straight and the unicycle saddle squeezed between your legs.

Continue riding forward with this half-pedal then freeze pattern. Avoid trying to regain balance by rocking the pedals back

Figure 3-4. Riding a half-pedal revolution forward with two helpers.

Figure 3-5. Dismounting to rear: (A) Stop with one pedal in a down position, release one hand from helper, and grasp saddle at front; (B) Step foot from upper-positioned pedal to ground behind the unicycle.

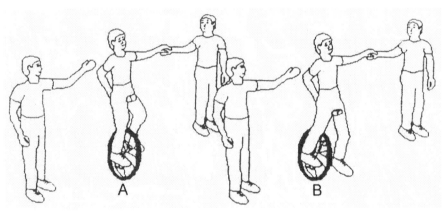

Figure 3-6. Dismounting forward: (A) Come to stop with one pedal in down position, release one hand from helper, and grasp back end of saddle; (B) Step foot from upper-positioned pedal forward to ground.

and forth or upper body motion, as this tends to confuse the helpers.

The freezing action should be done with the crank arms in a horizontal position. This makes it easy to start the next pedal action. Don't get stuck with one pedal down and one pedal up.

For dismounting (Figure 3-5), come to a complete stop with one pedal in the down position. Release one hand from a helper and grasp the forward end of the saddle. Step the foot from the upper-positioned pedal to the ground behind the unicycle. As you dismount off behind the unicycle, hold the unicycle by

the front of the saddle so that the unicycle does not fall.

Dismounting behind the unicycle is generally considered to be the most satisfactory method, although many beginners think coming off forward is correct. I suggest that you learn to dismount toward the rear of the unicycle first. But also try coming off forward (Figure 3-6) so that you know you can do it.

To dismount forward, come to a complete stop with one pedal in the down position. Release one hand from a helper and grasp the back end of the saddle. Step from the upper-positioned pedal to the ground in

Figure 3-7. Riding half-pedal revolution backwards with two helpers.

front of the unicycle. As you dismount forward, hold the unicycle up by the back of the saddle so that it does not fall to the ground.

Continue to practice mounting and riding forward with the help of two partners in the half-pedal and then freeze the pedal action pattern. Try to maintain good riding posture.

Gradually decrease the length of time in the freeze positions. The helpers should remain at your sides. Use less and less hand pressure with the helpers. Their main function at this point should be to prevent you from twisting and falling to the sides so that you can concentrate on learning the forward and backward balance pattern.

It is important have the hub of the unicycle move forward at the same speed as the saddle. Maintain good posture so that your upper body is a fixed part of the unicycle. Learn to maintain forward and backward balance by pedal action rather than upper-body movement.

I feel that it is important even at this beginning stage to be able to make balance corrections not only by pedaling forward, but also by pedaling backwards. If you start to lose balance backwards when you are not moving, the correct action is to pedal in a reverse direction. If you have spent years pedaling a bicycle in the forward direction only, it will take some practice to get used to pedaling backwards.

Practice riding half-pedal revolutions backwards with two helpers, freezing the pedals in the horizontal positions as was done previously with forward pedaling (Figure 3-7). Practice until you feel comfortable with the backward pedal action.

Then go back to forward riding, but from time to time work in some practice with backward pedaling. In this way, you will be learning both pedaling directions instead of forward only.

Continue practice with two helpers until you can ride forward with only light hand pressure on the two helpers. Also, make certain that you are maintaining good posture and making the balance corrections by pedal actions.

It may take less than an hour or a month

or more of daily practice to reach this stage. Before going on to the next stage, you should also be able to mount and dismount backwards and forwards with only light hand pressure with the helpers.

Riding with One Helper

The next step is to repeat the above practice exercises, except this time with only one helper (Figure 3-8). Continue to use the stop-block or curb for mounting, as was done previously (Figure 3-9). For riding forward, the helper should stand directly to your side. This can be to your right or left, whichever feels the most comfortable to you.

Begin by mounting the unicycle with the aid of the stop-block (Figure 3-9). Then ride forward, as was done previously. Maintain good riding posture and make forward and backward corrections by pedal action. When you are ready to dismount, dismount behind the unicycle, as detailed previously (Figure 3-10). The helper should remain directly to your side. Use hand pressure only with the helper's palm turned upward. Gradually decrease the hand pressure with the helper until

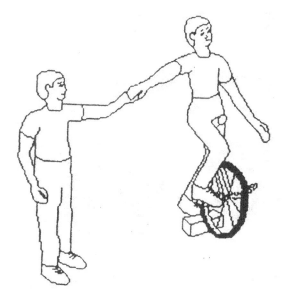

Figure 3-9. Mounting using stop-block and one helper.

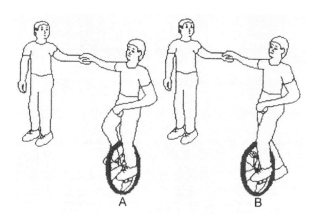

Figure 3-10. Dismounting to rear with one helper: (A) Come to stop with one pedal in down position and grasp back end of saddle; (B) Step foot from upper-positioned pedal rearward to ground.

you can solo. This may take less than an hour or a week or more of daily practice sessions.

Before going on to the next stage, you should be able to mount the unicycle with the aid of the curb or stop-block solo (with assistance from partner), ride with good posture and control for thirty feet or more, and then dismount to the rear of the unicycle with good control, catching the unicycle by the front of the saddle.

Figure 3-8. Riding half-pedal revolution forward with one helper.

From One Helper to Solo

The progression from using the one helper to riding solo should be gradual. After making half-pedal revolutions with freezing actions with the pedals in horizontal positions, try making full-pedal revolutions before freezing the action. Work up to the point where a number of pedal revolutions can be made continuously. When this can be done with only light hand pressure with the helper, try riding forward with brief hand releases with the helper (Figure 3-11). Have helper keep hand in position for grasping. Gradually work up to longer time periods of riding solo until you can ride with control for thirty feet or more (Figure 3-12).

Figure 3-12. Riding forward solo.

Figure 3-11. Riding forward with brief hand release from helper.

Use a similar procedure for learning to mount solo with a curb or stop-block (Figure 3-13) and dismount solo to the rear of the unicycle (Figure 3-14). The basic idea is to use the helper less and less until you can do the skills alone.

Also practice dismounting forward with one helper, gradually using helper less and less until you can do it alone (Figure 3-15).

You should also spend some time practicing backward riding with freezing actions after each half-pedal revolution with assistance from helper (Figure 3-16).

RIDING LONGER DISTANCES FORWARD

Once you can solo, as detailed above, the next step is to ride for longer distances. If you have mastered basic riding as detailed above, this should not be too difficult. Mount the unicycle using a curb or stop-block. Ride forward with a marker placed further than your previous record. This might be forty feet from the starting point. Ride with control to the marker and then dismount off behind the unicycle. Move the marker about ten feet further. Go back to the curb or stop-block and try for the new distance.

Continue until you can ride for 100 feet or more. Try to maintain a moderate pace with good control. Do not try to "race" at this point. At first, the unicycle will probably tend to wobble with the pedal action, but with practice this can be largely eliminated.

By this time, you may be wondering where your arms should be when you are unicycling. When you were riding with two helpers, you had a place to put your hands.

With one helper, you could put the free hand out like the one that went to the helper, or you could put it down at your side or somewhere in between. Riding solo, you have a choice of positions. To date, no arm positions have emerged as being "the correct" way to ride a unicycle, even for artistic competition. You may want to extend your arms outward like a tight wire walker, or place them casually to your sides, something like you do with natural walking.

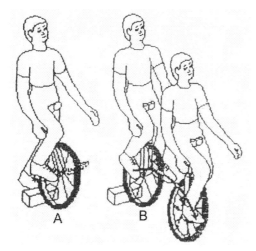

Figure 3-13. Mounting solo with stop-block: (A) Position unicycle against stop-block with one pedal back; (B) Mount unicycle and ride forward.

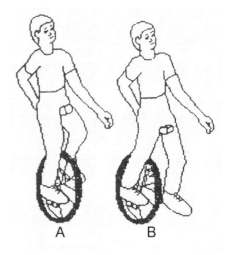

Figure 3-15. Dismounting forward solo: (A) Come to stop and grasp back of saddle; (B) Dismount forward.

Figure 3-14. Dismounting solo to rear: (A) Come to stop with one pedal down and grasp saddle; (B) Dismount to rear.

Figure 3-16. Riding half-pedal revolution backwards with one helper.

Chapter 4

BASIC RIDING SKILLS

Once you have learned basic forward riding as detailed in Chapter 3, you will want to go on to further challenges.

TURNING

After learning to ride forward in a straight line (more or less), the next step is to make turns (Figure 4-1). Generally by this time some turning has already been done. The object now is to learn to turn when and where desired with good control.

Turning (Figure 4-2) is basically leaning slightly in the direction you wish to turn and then twisting the unicycle slightly in that direction and pedaling forward so that the wheel of the unicycle is brought back under the center of gravity again. As a general rule, you should try to turn mainly by leaning, keeping arm swinging and upper-body twisting movement to a minimum.

Figure 4-1. Making a turn.

Figure 4-2. Basic turning.

First, mount the unicycle with aid of curb or stop-block, as was done previously, and ride forward. Then make a 45 degree turn over a distance of several feet. Then repeat with a 45 degree turn over a distance of several feet in the opposite direction.

Next, try 90 degree turns over a distance of several feet. Practice until you can make these turns in both directions with control.

Next, try half turns so that you reverse the direction of travel. The radius can be large at first, but gradually work down to a tighter turn. Then repeat with the turn in the opposite direction.

Always strive for complete control. Try to relax. Do not force the turns. Let a rhythmical lean do the work.

RIDING WITH A PARTNER

Once you have mastered basic riding, you are ready to try riding with a partner who has also mastered basic riding. It's even easier if your partner is a more advanced rider. In fact, an advanced rider can often substitute for a helper on foot for learning basic riding as detailed above in this chapter.

You can ride together with locked arms (Figure 4-3) and holding hands (Figure 4-4)

Figure 4-4. Riding forward with partner holding hands.

with both riders facing the same direction. You will probably want to learn both ways.

Both riders can mount separately and then ride side-by-side before joining arms or hands. Once arms or hands are joined, you can ride together in a straight line and make turns. Try to maintain good riding posture. Riding with a partner is usually easy once basic riding has been mastered; as the riders serve to help each other maintain balance.

Figure 4-3. Riding forward with partner with locked arms.

Figure 4-5. Riding in circle facing opposite directions with locked arms.

Also try riding with a partner in a circle facing opposite directions. To do this with locked arms (Figure 4-5), the riders come together from opposite directions riding forward and join arms. They then circle, each rider riding forward and following the same circle route on the opposite side of the circle. Finish by releasing arms and each rider going forward in opposite directions.

Figure 4-6. Riding in circle facing opposite directions holding hands.

To ride in a circle facing opposite directions holding hands (Figure 4-6), the riders come together from opposite directions riding forward and join hands. They then circle, with each rider following the same circle route on the opposite side of the circle. The riders should maintain outward pressure on the hand holding. Finish by releasing hands and each unicyclist riding forward in opposite directions.

MOUNTING

After you are able to mount alone with the aid of a stop-block or curb, the next step is to learn to mount in the open. Begin with two helpers. Position the unicycle with one pedal back (Figure 4-7). Straddle over the saddle and place foot on pedal that is back. Hold hands with the helpers, who should be directly to your sides. Apply downward pressure on the pedal and step the other foot upward to the forward pedal, using the backward motion of the unicycle wheel to draw the unicycle saddle up over the hub. Continue the backward pedal action until the pedal that was down and back is forward and the crank arms are in a horizontal position. Freeze the pedals in this position so that the helpers can easily get you in balance. Then ride forward.

An alternate method of pedal action for mounting is to begin as previously, except when you step the last foot from the ground to the upper pedal, catch the pedal at the top of the cycle and immediately begin forward pedal action. However, I suggest that you learn with the continued backward pedal action first. Then with continued practice, you can use only the amount of backward pedal action required to get the unicycle in the desired balance.

Continue practice until you can gain control over the unicycle wheel after mounting. Gradually use less and less hand pressure with the helpers. If when mounting you find that you are still off balance backwards when

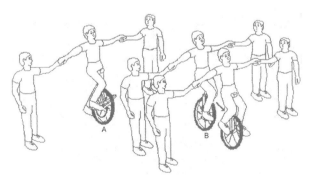

Figure 4-7. Mounting in open with two helpers: (A) Position for mounting; (B) Backward pedaling is used to bring rider in balance on unicycle before riding forward.

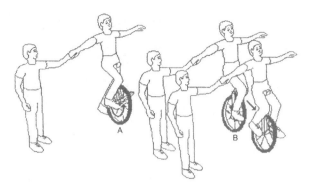

Figure 4-8. Mounting in open with one helper: (A) Position for mounting; (B) Pedal backwards to first horizontal pedal position before riding forward.

you reach the first horizontal pedal position, make an additional half pedal turn backwards to bring the unicycle into forward balance before riding forward. If you find that you are off balance forward when you reach the horizontal pedal position, start riding forward.

After you can mount with only light hand pressure from the two helpers, repeat the same practice exercises with one helper (Figure 4-8).

Continue practice, gradually using the helper less and less, until you can mount solo (Figure 4-9).

An alternate method for mounting is shown in Figure 4-10. The initial backward

Figure 4-9. Mounting solo in open.

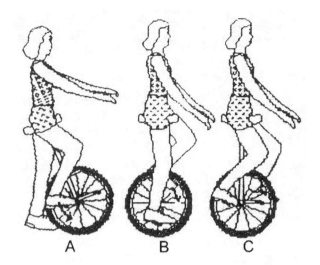

Figure 4-10. Alternate method for mounting: (A) Starting position; (B) Backward pedal action continues only to vertical position; (C) Forward pedal action to horizontal pedal position.

pedal action is continued only until the starting-foot pedal is in approximately the down position. The foot from the ground contacts the other pedal near the top of the cycle and immediately starts a forward pedal action.

More advanced riders often do something in between, back pedaling as required to place the unicycle in the desired position for the particular riding that is to follow.

The hands and arms can be in a variety of positions for regular mounting. The mounting is usually done with the hands free of the unicycle, but it is also possible to mount holding onto the saddle with one or both hands.

LEARNING WITH OPPOSITE-FOOT PATTERNS

In the above learning progression, it was suggested that you "place your best foot forward" for mounting and dismounting. This will serve well for most general and recreational riding. However, if you intend to go on to artistic riding, it is important to be able to do both mounting, dismounting, and half pe-

dal actions with the feet in the reversed positions. For example, if you had the right pedal back and your right foot on the pedal for mounting previously, you will need to learn mounting with the left pedal back and your left foot on the pedal. The same thing applies to making a half pedal turn backwards after mounting and to dismounting both backwards and forward from the unicycle.

To learn these, go back and repeat the learning steps with the stop-block or curb and helpers with the new foot patterns. Continue practice until you can do the skills solo.

CIRCLES AND OTHER PATTERNS

Riding in a continuous circle (Figure 4-11) is an extension of basic turning. Begin by making a large radius turn and continue in a circle pattern, following the same track each time around. The riding should be turning without noticeable twisting of the unicycle wheel in one spot. The pedal action should be smooth and continuous. Strive to maintain good riding posture.

Next, try riding in a continuous large radius circle in the opposite direction. Practice circles both directions, even though one di-

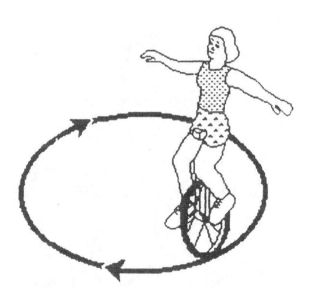

Figure 4-11. Riding forward in a circle.

rection will probably seem easier than the other. Many artistic riding skills require turning both directions.

Next try half-circle pattern (Figure 4-12) and figure-eight pattern (Figure 4-13). Other possibilities are serpentine and loop figures.

Figure 4-12. Half-circle pattern requires turning in both directions.

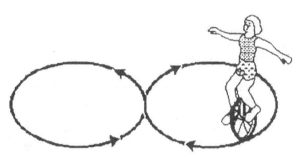

Figure 4-13. Figure-eight pattern.

RIDING BACKWARDS

If you have continued to practice half-pedal revolutions backwards with the helpers, as detailed in Chapter 3, you should be well on your way to learning to ride backwards (Figure 4-14) by this time. Begin with two helpers, as detailed in Chapter 3 for making half-pedal revolutions backwards. Try making a full pedal revolution before freezing the pedals in the horizontal position. After you have learned full pedal revolutions, try one-and-a-half revolutions, then two. Continue practice until you can ride backwards with continuous pedaling action with

Figure 4-14. Riding backwards.

the two helpers. Then gradually reduce the amount of hand pressure.

When you can ride backwards with good posture and control with light hand pressure with the two helpers, you are ready to try riding backwards with one helper. The helper should stand directly to your side but facing in the opposite direction to allow walking forward while you ride backwards. Maintain good riding posture. Ride backwards with a smooth pedaling action.

Gradually use less and less hand pressure until you can ride backwards solo. Maintain good riding posture and strive for smooth and continuous pedal action.

Solo backward riding can begin in a number of ways. One method is to mount against a fixed support, such as a wall or post, and then go into backward riding. Another method is to first ride forward, come to a stop with the pedals in a horizontal position, and then reverse the pedal direction to backward riding. More difficult is to mount in the open and then immediately start backward riding. Use a helper for learning this skill. Continue practice until you can do it solo.

IDLING

Idling is rocking back and forth in one place with half-pedal revolutions (Figure 4-15). There are two different patterns that can be used. One has the right foot making the lower half of the pedal cycle and the left making the upper half, as shown in Figure 4-15. The other pattern is the reverse of this, as shown in Figure 4-16.

Begin practice with one or two helpers or by using a wall or post as a hand support. The basic principle of idling is to lose balance forward, then pedal the wheel under the balance point until balance is lost backwards, then pedal the wheel back under the balance point until balance is lost forward. Practice with the helpers or support until you can do idling solo.

Learn idling with both foot patterns. This is important for learning more advanced skills.

When done correctly, the idling should

Figure 4-16. Idling with half-pedal revolutions with right foot making upper half of pedal cycle.

be with complete half-pedal revolutions. The motion should be rhythmical. The basic idea is to be off balance backwards, then make half-pedal revolution backwards to bring the unicycle to an off balance forward position. Then make half-pedal revolution forward to bring the unicycle back into an off balance backward position. Continue with a half-pedal revolution backwards. And so on.

After you can do idling solo, try to increase the number of back-and-forth cycles you can make in sequence. Or try to see how long you can continue. Gradually work up to more cycles or longer time periods. Be sure to practice both side patterns. Try to keep good riding posture and work for control.

Idling can be started from a mount, from forward riding, or from backward riding. Learn all three of these methods. Also try combinations, such as ride forward, go into idling and then ride backwards from the idling.

Figure 4-15. Idling with half-pedal revolutions with right foot making lower half of pedal cycle.

COMBINING SKILLS

The elementary artistic unicycling skills described above can be done in combinations to form sequences and routines. Sequences and routines are used for demonstrations, parade riding, performing, and artistic competition. Once you have mastered the individual skills, you can start putting them together in combinations. When you have reached this stage of learning, you will want to go on to more advanced skills and more difficult unicycles, such as giraffe models. A recommended source of information is this author's *The Complete Book of Unicycling, Second Edition*. It's available from **Amazon.com** in both printed and e-book formats. For more information about the author and his books, go to: **http://www.amazon.com/author/ jackwileypublications**.

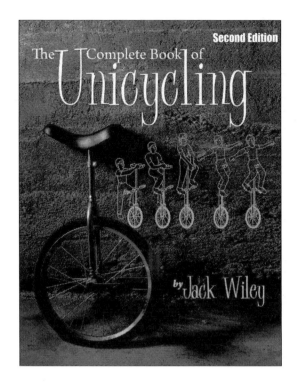

ABOUT THE AUTHOR

Jack Wiley has had a varied career. He traveled overland by buses and trains from the United States to Buenos Aires, Argentina, and returned by way of the Amazon; received his Ph.D. from the University of Illinois in 1968; did physiology research at the University of California at Santa Barbara; and lived aboard a sailboat for a number of years.

Dr. Jack Wiley first became interested in unicycling when he was in the seventh grade. A friend showed him the remains of a unicycle that had belonged to his uncle, a former professional stage performer. Jack Wiley purchased the unicycle and restored it with the help of a man at a bicycle shop.

He then learned to ride the unicycle, built other cycles, and worked up an amateur act. He performed in many shows in and around Fresno, California, including the Annual YMCA Circus.

Unicycling has remained an important part of his life since that time, and he has authored a number of books on the subject, including *The Complete Book of Unicycling* and *How to Build Unicycles and Artistic Bicycles.*

The author at an early age practicing for a YMCA circus.

For more information about Jack Wiley and his books, go to:
http://www.amazon.com/author/jackwileypublications

BOOKS BY JACK WILEY

For more information about the author and a complete list of his books, go to:
http://www.amazon.com/author/jackwileypublications.

The following books by Jack Wiley on unicycling, monocycling, circus skills, tumbling, balancing, diabolo, and other related subjects are available from **www. Amazon.com** in both printed and e-book formats:

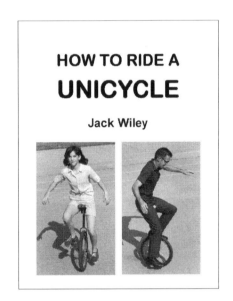

Jack Wiley, *How to Ride a Unicycle* **(39 pages in printed format).**

BESTSELLER

OVER 30,000 COPIES HAVE BEEN SOLD

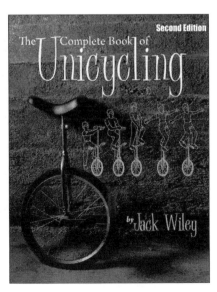

Jack Wiley, *The Complete Book of Unicycling: Second Edition* **(197 pages in printed format).**

BESTSELLER

OVER 20,000 COPIES HAVE BEEN SOLD

Jack Wiley, *How to Build Unicycles and Artistic Bicycles* **(87 pages in printed format).**

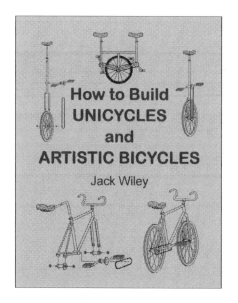

Jack Wiley, *Unicycles and Artistic Bicycles Illustrated* **(171 pages in printed format).**

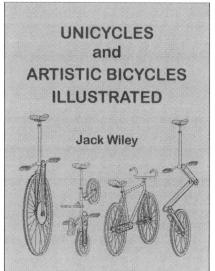

Jack Wiley, *On One Wheel: A Unicycling Autobiography* **(63 pages in printed format).**

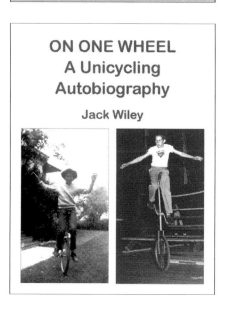

Jack Wiley, *Novelty Unicycling* (35 pages in printed format).

Jack Wiley, *The Ultimate Wheel Book* (37 pages in printed format).

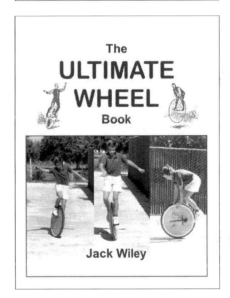

Jack Wiley, *Inside the Wheel: The Complete Guide to Monocycles* (39 pages in printed format).

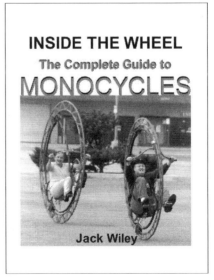

Jack Wiley, *Individual Tumbling, Acrobatics and Balancing* (69 pages in printed format).

Jack Wiley, *The Handstand Book: A Complete Guide to Standing on Your Hands* (63 pages in printed format).

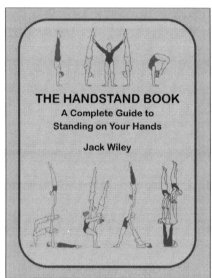

Jack Wiley, *Performing Basic Circus Skills* (69 pages in printed format).

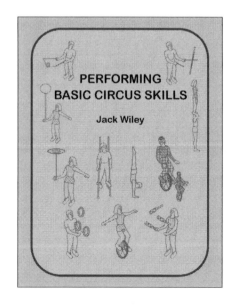

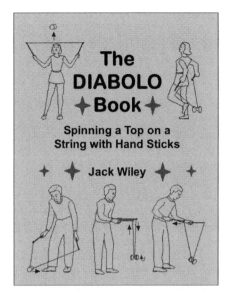

Jack Wiley, *The Diabolo Book: Spinning a Top on a String with Hand Sticks* (37 pages in printed format).

Jack Wiley, *How to Make Animated Toys and Whirligigs: Full-Size Patterns and Step-by-Step Instructions for Making Twenty Unique Animated Projects* (Available only in printed format; 239 pages).

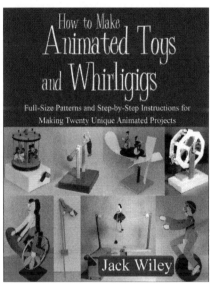

For more information about Jack Wiley and his books, go to:
http://www.amazon.com/author/jackwileypublications

Made in the USA
Las Vegas, NV
11 November 2021